Expanded Second Edition

REBORN IN THE U.S.A.

Personal Privacy — through — A New Identity

Trent Sands

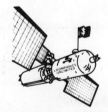

Loompanics Unlimited
Port Townsend, Washington

DISCLAIMER

This book in no way condones illegal activity! It is *your* responsibility to determine the legality of your actions. Further, because we have no control over the workmanship, materials, tools, methods, or testing procedures employed, we hereby disclaim any responsibility for consequences resulting from the fabrication or compounding of any item described in this book. We cannot and will not accept any responsibility for this information and its subsequent use. *This book is sold for informational purposes only!*

REBORN IN THE U.S.A., Expanded Second Edition
© 1991 by Loompanics Unlimited
All Rights Reserved
Printed in USA

Published by:
Loompanics Unlimited
PO Box 1197
Port Townsend, WA 98368

Loompanics Unlimited is a division of Loompanics Enterprises, Inc.

ISBN 1-55950-057-3
Library of Congress
   Catalog Card Number 90-064007

CONTENTS

INTRODUCTION

As Americans, we value our right of privacy very highly. The average person is concerned about the details of his personal life being made public. Information about his income, amount of savings, birthplace, marital status, and other personal data and much more is stored in many different computers that are accessible by many people. Most worrisome is that in the age of the computer all of this data can be quickly assembled into one file on any person.

The reality of today's world is that for a person to function without a lot of hassles (drive a car, cash checks, use credit) he must surrender most of his personal privacy. To drive, a person must have a license, which means a data file at the Motor Vehicle Department. When a person opens a bank account, another data file is created. If a credit card is applied for, a very detailed data file is created with a credit bureau. This file is updated monthly, and is available nationwide to almost anyone.

This book will show the reader how to regain his privacy through controlling what is stored in those various computers. The reader will enjoy all the benefits of society, but with one important difference: he will do it on his own terms. He will do so through the use of an alternate identity. He will keep his true identity private, and the computers will contain only the information he wants to provide.

There are already many books available on alternate identity. I have read most of them and tested the methods recommended. The problem with most of these books is that many key details are left out — critical details that can make the difference between success or failure. These other books also fail to approach alternate identity in terms of the overall identification system that now exists with the advent of the computer. On balance, I should say that these other books are excellent in many respects, and I refer the reader to these books throughout this one. This book is designed to be a "master guide" to the intricacies of creating a new identity that can withstand scrutiny. The other books will allow the reader to develop the expert knowledge in the various phases of creating an alternate identity.

After reading this book, read the others in the *Recommended Reading* chapter, and you will know almost everything about creating a new identity and, most importantly, how to avoid any screw-ups.

I should say a word about the motivation for this book. I do not advocate using these methods for criminal activity. This book is for the person who wants to regain his privacy. It is also for the person who, because of past misfortune or mistakes, wants to make a fresh start. The starting point is understanding the U.S. identification system.

- 1 -

THE U.S. IDENTIFICATION SYSTEM

Computers are everywhere and the computer never forgets. This is an important fact the new identity seeker should remember. Anytime you have contact with a clerk and a computer, the personal information you provide will be available to someone else for a long time. The identification system has as its foundation your birth certificate. This document validates that you were born in the United States at a certain place and location of specific parents.

The birth certificate acts as what is known as a "breeder document" which allows you to obtain a state identity card, drivers license, Social Security card, and other identification. Once these other documents are obtained, they become your primary source of official identity.

The motor vehicle department illustrates how the system works. In most states, your basic file at the motor vehicle department will contain:

- Full Name
- Birthdate
- Social Security Number
- Home Address
- Telephone Number
- Marital Status
- Height and Weight
- Eye and Hair Color
- Medical Data

Your file will also contain details on the documents you used to establish your identity. This is just your basic file, not including any traffic citations you may get. At first glance, the data seems harmless but it reveals much about you. If you live in a bad part of town, your address reveals that fact, possibly causing you to pay higher auto insurance rates. If you have a medical condition that affects your driving, it is common knowledge.

The most invasive data is your Social Security number, because it has nothing to do with the state function of issuing drivers licenses. Many states that do not put your Social Security number on the front of the license ask for it and store it in the computer. Why? Because with your Social Security number, numerous records about you are quickly available from other, allegedly separate computer files.

Legally, the Social Security number has only these uses: (1) for Social Security purposes and to establish worker enrollment in the program; (2) for federal income and withholding tax purposes — your Social Security number is used to positively identify your income tax return, and to report interest and investment income; (3) to establish eligibility for certain welfare programs, and (4) by the Selective Service system to identify draft-age men.

A law was passed banning the mandatory use of Social Security numbers by private organizations and most state government agencies. However, a clause in that law allows states that asked for the number before the law went into effect to continue to do so. The first step in understanding the identification system is to realize that your Social Security number has become a universal identifier that allows any record about you to be rapidly matched to other records. In effect, the Social Security number acts as a freeway with various exits that contain the details of your life. The health insurance industry provides the perfect example of how private organizations use the Social Security number.

Almost all insurance companies are members of an organization called the Medical Identification Bureau. The Bureau stores the medical and claim histories of everyone who has health or life insurance. The reason insurance companies request your Social Security number is so that the Bureau can index its files. This is necessary because many people have the same first, middle and last name, as well as identical birthdates. When you apply for insurance, you sign a blanket waiver allowing the insurance company total access to your medical history, and allowing them to share it with other insurance companies. This is why people who have been treated for certain illnesses find it impossible later on to purchase any insurance coverage.

This is bad enough, but the damage can extend much further. Many large companies that offer medical benefits to employees routinely send potential new employees' applications for screening by the Medical Information Bureau. If the application comes back with a notation that the applicant has a poor medical history, it can kill the job offer at once. The worst part is that the Medical Information Bureau is a private group that operates with very little regulation.

Another part of the identification system is the credit bureau. Anytime you apply for a credit card or a loan, your personal details and Social Security number are sent to the credit bureau. If you have had previous financial problems, they will return to haunt you. The information at the credit bureau is updated monthly. In addition to the personal data the credit bureau files contain, your current charge account balances and loan repayment history are shown. The credit bureau also monitors the local courthouse for any lawsuits or judgments against you. I recommend that every reader of this book obtain a copy of his credit file. More information on credit bureaus is contained in the book *Credit: The Cutting Edge* by Scott French, listed in the *Recommended Reading.*

Although credit bureau information has as its original purpose only to be a tool in assisting with loan decisions, its use has expanded greatly beyond this. Many companies run credit checks on new job applicants, and some landlords run credit checks on applicants for rental housing. A person who has had credit problems in the past can find that he cannot rent an apartment or obtain employment because of the information in the credit bureau files.

The identification system continues with the records your employer maintains, as well as telephone company records.

Telephone company records can be especially destructive of your privacy because the phone company knows who, when and where you call. Most telephone companies now request the Social Security number as part of getting new service.

From these different databanks, the government, or *any* investigator, can assemble a file on any citizen detailing the most private areas of his life. You will notice I did not mention arrest records, because compared to what can be learned from other files, they yield relatively little — especially in the case of the law-abiding citizen who has never been arrested.

The federal government has been encouraging states to do more filing and cross-indexing of state records using the Social Security number. This would allow the states to create a central file on a citizen for all state-held information. This is possible because most states have no laws prohibiting this, and the loophole in the before-mentioned law about Social Security number usage as an identifier. A typical state "central index" would be cataloged by name and Social Security number. In the file for each citizen would be headings for state income tax returns, motor vehicle registrations, driver licensing, state court actions in regard to the individual, etc. Remote terminals in state offices would allow any state clerk to access the database. This system would allow the federal government to escape the legal prohibitions against creating a federal central index on all citizens by using the states as proxies.

An example of how this would work is the new federal law that allows states to revoke drivers licenses of people who have been convicted of federal drug offenses. After a conviction, the federal government gives the convict's name and Social Security number to the states to search for that person's drivers license. Under the central index scheme it becomes very easy to do so. I should mention that this extends to other programs as well, such as public assistance, which are administered by the states.

As we have seen, the identification system has an enormous reliance on the Social Security number because it is the only totally unique identifier people have, other than fingerprints. In the remaining chapters, we will deal with each phase of the system and show you how to defeat it.

- 2 -
THE
MAIL DROP

The first step is to establish an address and telephone number apart from your own. This address will become the "home" of your new identity. In every city there are mail forwarding services. For a monthly fee, these agencies will allow you to use their street address for your mail. For an additional amount, they often offer a telephone message service. The reason for establishing a telephone number and address at a mail service is that, when you obtain the documents for a new identity, there is nothing by way of an address to link the real you with your new identity. The one sticky part of a mail drop is opening your account. If it is done wrong, a link between you and your new identity will be created.

How to use a mail drop service can be found in the book *How To Use Mail Drops For Privacy and Profit* listed in the *Recommended Reading* on page 82. Keep some things in mind as you select your mail drop. Your mail drop should be in a residential area, not downtown. Get telephone message service as well — it makes your new identity much more credible. People without a telephone number are suspect. Also, consider the type of neighborhood your mail drop is in. A nice, middle class part of town is perfect. Always try to get a mail drop with 24 hour access. This allows you to pick up your mail from your box at any time in total privacy. Usually you will use the street address of the service, with your box number given as a suite or apartment number.

Opening your mail drop can leave traces, as this example will illustrate. A few years ago I wrote to a mail forwarding service in another city requesting information, using my real name. A week later I received the application form along with the box number I was to use. I rented the box under a different name, filling out the application in this name. Later when I went to pay my account at this mail service, I caught a glance at their files. Still in the file was my original letter to them with my real name on it. To this mail operator's credit he did protect customers' privacy. But for the alternate identity seeker leaving something serious behind, my error could have been fatal.

When you have located the mail service you want, call them, but do not write. They will send you the information by mail. Do not use your real name, but give your real address. Whoever answers the telephone will jot down your address on a memo pad and send the information. The memo will be thrown out at the end of the day. No trace is created. What you will receive in the mail is a short form from the mail service operator and an imposing looking form from the Post Office. Fill out the form from the mail service operator with a typewriter with your phoney name and bogus address.

Photocopy it and sign it with an illegible signature. On the postal service form you will be asked to give the name and number from two pieces of identification, your current address, and a bunch of other information. Do the same as before, photocopy it and sign it. You will submit the photocopies. Pay for your service with a money order, not with a check or credit card. That just creates a trail back to you.

You will not want mail forwarding. You take in the application in person. Odds are you will not be asked for any identification because the paperwork is already done. A good story to use if you are asked for some identification is to say that you are dropping off the papers for your uncle. Most mail drop operators will not ask a thing. They will give you your box and lobby key, and this will be the only time you will go into the mail service during business hours. Most mail drops will allow you to get mail under any name as long as you use the correct box or suite number.

The next thing to do is start getting some mail at your mail drop. It will look suspicious if for two months you get no mail, then suddenly start getting mail from different state vital statistics bureaus. Sign up for a catalog or magazine subscription. Just make sure that you do not subscribe to any specialized magazines that the old you used to receive. An investigator could find you through the subscriber list.

- 3 -
THE
BIRTH
CERTIFICATE

In many ways, this chapter is the heart of the book. To obtain any government-issued identification, you usually must provide your birth certificate. There are two methods of obtaining a new birth certificate. The first method is known as the "infant identity method" and involves using a birth certificate of someone who died at a very young age. The second method is to create an entirely new identity through a false birth certificate. Each method has its advantages and problems but, if done properly the problems with either method can be eliminated.

The infant identity method requires you to find the identity of a dead child. You can do this by going to a graveyard or by going through old newspapers. What you should not do under any circumstance, which is what many of the other books recommend, is to look up a plane or train crash to find a dead child's identity to use. Why? Because many other identity changers have already requested these birth certificates many times before. If one particular birth certificate is requested too often, the state vital statistics bureau will flag it for nonrelease, or trigger an investigation of why it is being requested so often. The other pitfall for the identity changer is what is called cross-referencing of birth and death records. Usually this will occur at the county level, but it is also done at the state level in many places. When a person dies in the same county of their birth, the county registrar will stamp "deceased" on the person's birth certificate. In statewide cross-referencing, a similar process will occur at the state vital statistics office for all people who were born and died in that state. There are two possible ways around this problem.

Look through old newspapers for a child who died in an isolated incident. Pick a child who would be around your age today. First write for the death certificate. The death certificate will let you know if the child was born in the same county or state of death. You will write for the death certificate in the name of the father or mother of the late child. You can then request the birth certificate. If the state only cross-references on a countywide basis, the identity is okay to use if the death occurred in another county. If the state cross-references on a statewide basis, you should find another child. However, if this particular identity is ideal for your needs, the following will often work.

In most states both the central vital statistics bureau and local county office issue birth certificates. If statewide cross-referencing of birth and death records exist, often it is only done at the central state office, and will appear on birth certificates issued from that office. A way around this problem is to write to both the county and state offices for the certificate. You will then have a definitive answer. Another loophole is that states that cross-reference only began doing this with records starting at a certain date. There have been too many people born and already dead to go back very far. *The best protection is to find a child who was born in one state and died in another.* Another possible loophole is many large cities operate independent vital statistics offices for all births and deaths within city limits. Odds are statewide or county-wide cross-referencing will not affect them. To find out, call or write on a suitable letterhead, and ask directly if cross-referencing is in place. I refer you to an additional book, *Birth Certificate Fraud,* listed in the *Recommended Reading.*

I cannot overstress the fact that you should not attempt to build your new identity on a child who died in a well-publicized disaster. The local county registrar may remember the incident because he had to issue the death certificates. Or the registrar may even know the late child's parents. The major reason is the one given earlier: Other identity changers may have already used these identities because that method is so widely recommended in other books. The sad but common child death is best for the new identity seeker.

The second method is to create an entirely new identity. I prefer this method because the death of a child is always tragic, and it rubs me wrong to take advantage of it. Done properly, creating your own identity will work just as well, and it has the advantage that you can pick your own birthdate, name, and other data. You must first get hold of a birth certificate. Never purchase one from a mail order company. Almost all of them are junk, and any bureaucrat will recognize them at once.

Look up old birth notices in a newspaper from the state you wish to be reborn in. Write for a birth certificate. This way you know what the actual state document looks like. This is very important because people move around. If you are in Washington state attempting to obtain a drivers license with a Kansas birth certificate, the clerk might be from Kansas. Or the clerk may have just seen a Kansas birth certificate. Your foresight ensures that the document you present looks authentic.

Now that you have a birth certificate, you must decide the particulars of your new identity. You should start with a blank sheet of paper and list:

- Full Name
- Birthdate
- Birthplace
- Father's Birthplace
- Father's Name
- Mother's Maiden Name
- Mother's Birthplace

You must invent all of this. Choose a common name, but not Smith, Miller or Jones. Choose other data that you can easily remember. After you have compiled all the data, you will create a blank of the original certificate, and insert the new particulars. The procedures to follow are laid out in exact detail in the book *Counterfeit I.D. Made Easy,* listed in the *Recommended Reading.*

Although the birth certificate is the crucial document, alone it will not allow you to obtain other government identification. A person with only a birth certificate is suspect. You must have some other identification to support your birth document. This identification is called secondary, back-up, or supportive identification. It is extremely easy to obtain.

- 4 -
GETTING
IDENTIFICATION
CARDS

Your birth certificate must be accompanied by other documents so that you appear to be an upstanding citizen. This is the only time that you will make use of mail order and self-made identification cards.

The first piece of supportive identification you will need is a Social Security card. Not the real one from Uncle Sam (that will come later) but a mail-order one. Mail-order Social Security cards are one of the few times where mail order identification is just as good as the real thing. The reason for this is over the years many different types of Social Security cards have been issued by the government. The design is basically a blue bordered card with the words "SOCIAL SECURITY" at the top. Your Social Security number is underneath on a white background, along with your printed name and a signature space. Some editions of the card have a seal on it, others do not. Another reason mail order Social Security cards work so well is that most people do not carry the card on their person. Most people just know their number. You should read the book *I.D. By Mail,* listed in the *Recommended Reading.* This book contains the names and addresses of issuers of privately made identity cards. At least one issuer sells Social Security cards that resemble the real ones extremely well.

The next step involves creating your new Social Security number. Every state has a certain three-digit series that heads the number assigned to it. You can find out what these series are by consulting Appendix Three. *Understanding U.S. Identity Documents* is an excellent reference to this. It is listed in the *Recommended Reading.*

Some other pointers are necessary. First, if you are playing the role of being a newcomer to the state, it will make no sense to the clerk if your Social Security number is one that state's residents would have. Secondly, if you choose a Social Security number from a large state, like New York, or California, the chances are much greater that you will accidently use a real number issued to someone else. So pick a series from a small state. North and South Dakota come to mind, as well as Wyoming, Alaska, etc.

The next step is to get a second piece of identification that has a picture on it. The way I suggest requires a bit of effort, but it will give you a solid piece of identification. Look in the phone book for a secretarial service and call a few. Your story will be that you run a business out of your home and you would like a better image. A secretarial service can rent you a private telephone line which they will answer in your company name, and also receive and forward company mail for you. This is all arranged on a monthly basis for a modest fee. After you have arranged this, go to a quick print shop and have them run off letterhead stationary, envelopes, and blank employee identification cards. See the book *Counterfeit I.D. Made Easy* for the layout of the card. The printer will be glad to help and your request will not raise any questions. To make your employee I.D. card acceptable as hard identification, it should contain the following:

- Employee Name
- Employee Number
- Job Title
- Height and Weight
- Date of Issue
- Signature
- Company Name
- Company Address
- Company Phone Number

You will need to get some passport-size photos made for the card. Once you have these, glue the photograph onto the card, sign it, and get it laminated in heavy plastic. To fill out your supply of secondary identification cards, I suggest a library card and especially a voter registration card. In many states a voter registration card is a very good looking piece of secondary identification. Another piece of secondary identification would be a student card from a local college. Register for one class, and you get the card. Now you are ready for the motor vehicle bureaucrats.

I recommend you first apply for a state identity card. This will give you a chance to see how the system works, and it will make it easier to get the drivers license later on. The reason for this is you will already have a piece of "their" identification and so you will face much less scrutiny. The state identity card is easier to get because it is often the first piece of state-issued identification a person gets. Before you go, sit down and review for hours all the details of your new identity. This way, when you go before the motor vehicle people, you will be calm and cool. Once you have passed this test the hardest hurdle is over.

Here are a few tips on getting your drivers license. While you are at the motor vehicle department getting the state identity card, ask for a copy of the drivers education manual. Make sure you study it so you can pass the test. Go back to the motor vehicle department two weeks later and take the written test. You will be given a learners permit. Practice driving the way you must for the road test. Under no circumstances take the road test in your own car. In many states the license plate and vehicle registration details of the car used for the driving test are recorded and go into your file. Needless to say, this provides a direct link between the old and new identity. The best way is to arrange for one lesson and the driving test to be taken in a car from a driving school.

I cannot overstress the need for you to be totally comfortable in your new identity. Remember that Americans move around a lot. If your new birth certificate says you are from Cincinnati, Ohio, you better know about Cincinnati chili. The best way to learn about your new hometown is to start with encyclopedia articles about the state and city. Then write to the state's tourist bureau for more information, or to the auto club. Another excellent way to start is by reading the newspaper from your new hometown. Often university libraries or larger public libraries have out-of-town newspapers. Know how the local sports teams are doing, the governor of the state, and who the mayor of your new hometown is. Never pick as your new background places that are totally the opposite of yourself. The watchword of a new identity is credibility. If you are from Boston, do not pick a southern city as your new hometown. It just will not carry well. Stick with backgrounds you can assume with confidence.

We now turn to Social Security cards. Your bogus Social Security card was intended as only an interim step. You should get a real Social Security card for two reasons. The first is, if you intend to live and work under your new identity permanently, you will want to get your Social Security benefits. The second reason is a nonexistent Social Security number will eventually cause problems. As your employer sends in Social Security taxes to a nonexistent account, the computer will one day spit out that your number is invalid. Your employer will receive a letter asking him to obtain the correct number. Another problem is banks must obtain your number so they can report the interest you earn. This information is matched up with your income tax return. The last thing you need is trouble with the Internal Revenue Service.

Getting a Social Security number is now pretty simple. The federal government, in an attempt to give everyone a number, has made it easier for the privacy seeker. For a person to claim a dependant child over age five as an income tax deduction, the I.R.S. requires these children to have Social Security numbers. This means hundreds of thousands more applications for Social Security numbers are being made, especially early in the year, before tax time. Another loophole is that juveniles can apply by mail. No mention is made on your Social Security card of your age. So apply as a juvenile. Regardless of the method used in establishing your new identity, the procedure is the same. Simply take a blank copy of your new birth certificate, and using the methods referred to in the book *Counterfeit I.D. Made Easy,* change the relevant data so you are seventeen or younger. Make sure the other information fits, such as the age of your "parents." Apply at the end of the month. Everything will appear in order and within six weeks you will have your new card. Later, when you are ready to collect your Social Security, you will get your "file error" corrected without any trouble.

The last piece of identification the identity changer may want is a passport. If you use the infant identity method in a state that does not cross-reference vital records, you will have no problem. The passport challenge is harder, but not impossible, if you have created a new person. The passport office is very aware of identity fraud, because over the years so many people have gotten false passports. I suggest you read the books *The Passport Agent's Manual* and the relevant sections of the aforementioned *Birth Certificate Fraud.*

Most passport applications are processed routinely unless the passport agency clerk has reason to suspect otherwise. I recently applied for a passport under my own name at a passport agency. The clerk took my birth certificate, examined it, and wrote down the file and birth numbers from it on the back of the application. It was then returned to me. She then requested my drivers license as proof of identity. Three days later I had my passport. There was not enough time for the passport office to have written to verify my birth certificate. If something had been suspect, they would have retained my birth certificate and returned it with the passport. After watching what the clerk wrote on the back of the form, a number of important points became clear.

First, *never* apply for a passport using the bogus birth certificate method at a post office or state court authorized to handle passport applications. As you will note from reading the before-mentioned book on passports, these applications require that the birth certificate be submitted, and when the State Department people receive these applications, they are scrutinized.

Second, when you apply, make sure that your phoney birth certificate is created on a state issued birth form, and not one from a local county registrar. The reason for this is that county-issued birth documents usually only carry a local registrar's file number and not a state-issued birth number. Also, county certificates will often have a different format and seal. The state birth number is coded to indicate the year and county of birth. So when you create a new identity, let the county, date and type of birth remain the same. Change only your name and that of the parents. My suspicion is the passport agency people perform a quick check on the validity of a birth certificate by comparing those numbers on the certificate with a listing of representative numbers from all the states. The benefits to the passport office are clear. It allows them to catch most would-be phoney passport holders, because they know nothing of this detail, at a very low cost. To verify every application on a timely basis would be very expensive, and delay passports for months.

Never apply for passports in certain cities. Examples would be New York, El Paso, Los Angeles, etc. These cities have had a lot of fraudulent applications, and they routinely verify a certain percentage of applications. Do not apply for a passport until you have been in your new identity for at least a year. If all of a passport applicant's identification is less than a year old it can be a tip-off to the clerk. If you do travel overseas on your new passport, take some precautions.

When a person's passport is lost or stolen, usually all of his other identification is stolen as well. If you request an emergency passport at the overseas consulate, the odds are very good that the consulate will wire your state of birth for a copy of your birth certificate. If you are using a real birth certificate, no problem. But if you are using the other method, you are in big trouble because your birth record is non-existent.

Take this precaution. Make a photocopy of your passport. Keep this with your new birth certificate. When you arrive at your destination, keep the passport photocopy, the birth certificate, and an identification card in a safe place. Should your passport be stolen, you can go to the consulate with this evidence and quickly get a new one. The consulate will send the details of your old passport and birth certificate/ identification to the passport agency. They will match with the information given on the passport application. They will cancel your old passport and issue you a new one. The consul will compliment you on your foresight.

Your new identity is almost complete. However, a few areas remain to be dealt with. These are banking and credit, as well as employment.

- 5 -

BANKING
AND
CREDIT

Having a bank account is necessary for just about everyone. The proper set-up and use of a bank account is crucial for the identity changer. Your bank account can reveal the intimate details of your life, but the identity changer must have a checking and savings account because a person without them is suspect. Throughout this book I have stressed the need to pay for certain things with money orders. The reason for this is a law called the Bank Secrecy Act which dictates the operation of every deposit-taking financial institution in the United States.

The Bank Secrecy Act says the details of every non-cash transaction through your bank account must be recorded and saved by the bank. Every check you write or deposit, any account transfer you make, must be recorded. In a matter of minutes any investigator can find out how, where and when you spend your money. A sloppy identity changer can destroy the value of all his efforts by not paying close attention to details here.

Here is a simple example. One day you are short of cash. You write a check on the bank account in your real name and deposit it into the account in the name of your new identity. A record is generated in your new bank as to the writer, amount and bank and account number of the check you deposited. At the bank the check is drawn on, a record is created as to who you sent the check to. A clear link between the old and new identities has been established. Another example is paying with a check when you are requesting various state's birth certificates. The check you pay the fee with will be saved by your bank for a few years. An investigator who sees you have been sending checks to the vital statistics bureau would quickly conclude you are seeking a new identity.

The lesson here is: One screw-up can be fatal, especially if someone is looking for you. You should approach your bank account with a ten foot pole. Take the attitude that you want your bank account to reveal nothing about you. You must open the account properly. Go to a bank that is actively seeking new accounts. You will open your new account with cash, about 300 dollars. You will have your drivers license, state identity card, and other identification at the ready. You make small talk with the clerk and in ten minutes it is over. After this initial contact you should never have to visit the branch again. You will do all your banking through the automated teller machine. You will never write a check on your checking account. When you need cash you will get it from the machine. You will pay your bills by making cash withdrawals and purchasing money orders at a store or post office. Never purchase a money order at your bank because often a notation will be put into the bank's records that you withdrew so much money and then purchased a money order. If you are working under your new identity, cash your paychecks at the bank they are drawn on and then deposit cash or a money order into your account.

You may be wondering why I recommend you treat your paychecks in this manner. When you opened your new account you gave as your employer the company front we set up earlier. You probably gave yourself a nice job title as well. If in reality you are working as a waiter, it will appear odd that you are depositing payroll checks from a local restaurant.

The next facet to banking is credit. After you have opened your new bank account, open an account at a local credit union. Most cities have open bond credit unions that allow anyone to join who lives in the area. Another way to qualify for credit union membership is to enroll for a class at a local college. Each month, make a deposit of one hundred dollars into your credit union account. After you have 500 dollars in your account, approach the manager and tell him you would like to borrow 500 dollars secured by your savings account. It will be easy, and once you have gotten the loan you will have a file at the local credit bureau. The information on that file will be the information you gave when you opened your credit union account, or on any additional paperwork required for the loan. More information on the credit system and how you should create your credit profile is available in the book *Credit: The Cutting Edge.*

Here is what you should not do. You will see advertisements that guarantee you will get a credit card in return for a secured deposit at their bank. The interest rates and annual fees on these cards are very high. They can also poison your credit record later on if you want to get unsecured credit cards or loans. Most bankers know who the banks are that issue these cards, and the bankers also know that the people who get credit cards this way have probably had credit problems in the past, and are poor credit risks. Some banks will automatically turn you down if you have one of these accounts, even if all your payments are on time. The same is true for finance companies. A finance or loan company account on your credit record hurts you because bankers know people go to finance companies when they cannot borrow from their local bank. It will take longer, but go the credit union route to establish your credit. A good time to apply for credit cards is in early to middle November. Credit standards are relaxed so people can go into debt for Christmas.

Once you have a credit card, remember that it provides yet another avenue to learn much about you. Only use your credit card for transactions that you feel are harmless if someone else knew about them. For transactions that you want to keep private, take a cash advance on your credit card and pay for the item or service with the money. After you get your first credit card, apply for another one every two months. Within a year, you will have unlimited credit.

- 6 -

EMPLOYMENT

Employment can be a real problem for the privacy seeker who wants to work under his new identity. By using the methods in this book your new identity will be solid, but employment requires additional backup. I suggested before that you use a secretarial service that will answer a private telephone line in a company name of your choosing. This gave the necessary support for your employee identity card and allowed you to present the picture of a gainfully-employed individual when you opened a bank account or applied for credit.

If you are looking for relatively simple low level work, your cover company will do just fine. When you fill out the employment application you will list as your past employer your cover company along with the telephone number and the name of your "supervisor." When your potential employer calls your secretarial service they will answer in the company name and tell the caller that the "supervisor" is out. They will take a message and have your "supervisor" return the call. Of course, *you* will actually be returning the call, playing the role of the supervisor. For most low level ordinary jobs, this is all the reference checking that is done. However, you must once again pay close attention to the details. Make sure the secretarial service has the name of the supervisor. The day after you put in a job application you must be sure to call the secretarial service every hour to get the messages.

For the identity changer who is seeking higher level work, much more is needed, because a background check is often required. This may be because bonding is necessary, or a security clearance is required. One book on alternate identity suggests if a job requires any kind of background check, the new identity seeker must forget it. This is false. In only a few cases, such as a job requiring a Defense Department security clearance, is this the case. The best way to illustrate this is to show why a new identity changer will be caught if he tries to get a job requiring a Defense Department security clearance.

To obtain a Defense Department security clearance, a person must complete a series of forms that detail one's work history, personal life history and financial status. In addition, waivers must be signed giving the government access to your medical records and the applicant must provide copies of his birth certificate, drivers license, and Social Security card. For the sake of argument we will assume that you have been living under your new identity for two years, and that you have made legitimate references in the manner of employment and personal friends. We will further say that you have never been arrested and fingerprinted.

The first step in any security clearance investigation is what is known as a passive or negative investigation. Essentially, this involves making sure that you are not a criminal and have not been convicted of a crime. Your name and personal particulars will be run through the FBI computer database. You will come back clean. The next part of the passive investigation will involve running a credit check on you through a credit bureau, reviewing your medical records, and verifying your birth certificate. We will also assume that you have used a real birth document to create your new identity. So your birth certificate will check out. They will also check with the IRS to make sure you paid your taxes last year. This will conclude the passive investigation which you will pass with no trouble. The next stage is the field investigation.

On the paperwork that you filled out you will have had to give the names of various people you have known over the years who can vouch for you. This is where your new identity will be revealed. When FBI agents talk to your references, the people will say good things about you. But the question the FBI man will always ask is, "About how long have you known John Doe?" Everyone will answer about two years. This "break" will arouse suspicion at once. The next thing the agent will do is check his sources again. Your credit file will be about two years old, and so will your employment history. A more detailed check with the IRS and Social Security people will reveal only two years of tax returns filed under your Social Security number. The warning bells will sound and a possible counter espionage investigation will begin.

The problem with any new identity is it had to be set up at some point in time. This is the reason the Soviet Union will take the risk of trying to bribe an American who works in a sensitive position, instead of getting a KGB agent hired at a defense plant. But the good news is: a careful identity changer can pass almost all *passive* investigations, especially those done at the state level. For example, many states require that child care workers, school teachers, etc., have background checks. States do not have access to the databanks the federal government does, and usually do only passive investigations. Usually, fingerprints are not required. However, there is a way around the fingerprint problem if you have been arrested. It is possible for any person to have additional sets of fingerprints. The technique is described in the book *How Intelligence Agents Change Their Fingerprints,* listed in the *Recommended Reading.* However, I suggest you use an alternative set of fingerprints even if you have never been arrested. The reason is later on, if you decide to go back to your true identity and are fingerprinted for any reason, your real name will come back as being an alias. This can cause a lot of problems for you, as well as the obvious fact that it destroys the value of your new identity.

You can safely apply for almost all state government jobs, and most routine federal civil service positions. You can also apply for jobs that require routine bonding such as bank tellers. The places to avoid are working for defense contractors or police agency jobs. But you can work for a company that does defense work, if it is in a non-defense subsidiary. Only the people who work in the defense part of the company must have clearance.

Another remaining problem is the new identity seeker who has university degrees and wishes to continue working in his field. The problem is that your educational records are in your old name. There are a variety of ways around this problem. The first way is to take your university transcripts and blot out the old data and insert your new name. When you apply for the job, submit your transcript with a resume. Most of the time, when an employer gets a transcript with a resume, all he does is call or write the former employer. A good employment reference gets you the job with no further checking. The problem with this is many larger companies require potential new hires to sign a transcript release form, allowing the employer to write to the university directly and request the transcript. One way around this is to base your new identity upon someone who has your kind of qualifications.

The first step is to contact the alumni associations of some universities and order a copy of their alumni book for whatever department or division you would have graduated from. The alumni director will have the name, addresses, class year and degree/major of the graduate. You could then call potential prospects and tell them you are calling from the alumni association and are updating your files. You would then get the birthdate and former student number of the individual. After you have done this, you can write for his transcript. You can then use his name and background as a basis for your new identity. But you must use some caution.

First, make sure the individual is not living in your state or the future state you will live in. Make sure you do not apply for a professional license in the state he is in. Always reverse the order of the middle and first names of the individual. After that, you would go about as before, building up the identification using the techniques already described. The obvious question is: will the computer realize that there are two of "you"? The answer is no, because you are only using his name and a few other particulars as a shell. By changing the order of the names, as well as having a different address, social security number and other data, you are an entirely different person to the computer. Think of how many "John Millers" have graduated in Electrical Engineering from a large university in a given year? Now think how many John Millers who are Electrical Engineers have the same birthdate. Quite a few. As long as you are only using his identity as a "shell" and are living in another state, you will have no problems. More on this is available in the book *How To Steal A Job,* listed in the *Recommended Reading.*

Another option for the professional is to use your company front and run an employment ad in the local paper for the type of job you want. In the ad you will request that the applicant submit his transcripts with the resume. In the ad, offer a salary at least twenty percent higher than normal for that job. Within two weeks you will be flooded with replies. I suggest that in the long term you get new, legitimate degrees in your new name if at all possible. There are many options, be it night school, correspondence courses, etc. Or you could use your purloined transcript to get admitted into graduate school and earn a real higher degree.

- 7 -
THE BIRTH CERTIFICATE PROCESS

The birth certificate is the foundation document for a person's identity in any country. In previous chapters, we have examined how a birth certificate acts as a "breeder" document to obtain other identification, but we have never really looked at the whole system of birth records in the United States.

The United States is unique among nations because our birth recording system is highly decentralized and is done on many levels. There are a minimum of four types of birth records issued in the United States today. In some states the authorities have attempted to make it more difficult for a new identity seeker to obtain state maintained birth records. But often in these same states the other three types of birth records are equally acceptable, provided they are presented in the proper context.

This chapter will examine these various birth records, who maintains them, and their overall acceptability.

Today most people are born in a hospital. I say most, but it certainly is not universal everywhere. In some states over half of all births occur outside the hospitals. We will use the hospital birth as an example, because it allows us to see the birth recording process at work in all its facets.

When a child is born at a hospital, the attending physician or nurse will fill out a short piece of paper with the time and sex and type of birth. Later on, after everything is finished in the recovery room, the doctor will fill out that particular hospital's standard birth certificate form. This form will have the name of the hospital, the location of the hospital, and some very basic information on it. The parents' name and ages at the time of birth are shown, along with the child's name, sex, and time of birth. At the bottom are places for the doctor's signature and the signature of a witness. The hospital's own seal will usually be on this form.

Once this form is completed, a photocopy is made of it and notarized, and the original is given to the parents. At this point in time, this *hospital-generated* birth certificate is the only legal record of this child's birth. Later on the hospital will send the notarized photocopy of the birth record to the county recorder's office. Upon receipt of this notarized copy of the hospital birth record, the county recorder will enter the birth record into the birth records book for the county for that month. Then, in some places, the county recorder will send out a state issued birth certificate to the parents. On a monthly or quarterly basis the county recorder will forward to the central state vital statistics bureau a listing of all births that occurred during that period. So, for a period of many months, the infant would not have his birth record on file at the central state vital statistics office. The notarized photocopy of the hospital birth record is generally destroyed by the local registrar once the birth has been entered into the records book. Often there is a delay of up to a month before even the local registrar enters the birth into the records book.

What should be clear here is that almost everyone born in a hospital actually has *two* birth certificates, each of which has legal status. The hospital record of birth is the only birth record the person has until such time as the county recorder enters the birth. Very often what mail order companies sell as birth certificates are hospital type birth records. Many people never get a state issued birth record, and the hospital issued record is their birth record. This can occur in many ways. Any doctor or nurse or, in some states, midwives who regularly assist in births will have a supply of these hospital-type birth certificates. They will also possess their own stamp or embossing tool to certify the document. This is particularly true in rural southern states.

Let's say a midwife has just attended the birth with her assistant. After the birth is done, she would sit down and complete the certificate with all the pertinent details. After her assistant or other witness signed it, she would then stamp or seal it and place her signature on the form. Then often she will tell the newborn's parents that they need to take this certificate to the local county registrar as soon as possible so the birth is registered with the state. Oftentimes even when a doctor or nurse attends a home birth, and under most state laws doctors and nurses are required to send birth notification to the county registrar, it does not happen. This is such a common occurrence that you will find that most state and federal government agencies will accept a hospital birth record in lieu of a state issued birth certificate.

Now, before you run out and purchase a hospital style birth certificate to build a new identity around, let's look at some subtle facts here. First of all, a person only receives a hospital birth record *once* — at the time of birth. Generally hospitals dispose of their copies of the birth record after the birth record has been registered with the county clerk. Most hospitals will keep a list of all babies born there, as often doctors and midwives do, but the actual paperwork is disposed of after a year or so.

If you were to present a freshly minted and sealed hospital birth record to a motor vehicle department bureaucrat, his suspicion would be aroused. Because that birth certificate should be at least *sixteen* years old, it should look it. Hospitals cannot issue duplicate copies of the birth record because the original is no longer available. Almost all federal government identity bureaucrats know this and so do most state identity bureaucrats. If you wish to use such a certificate, we will illustrate a way around this problem later on.

The third type of birth certificate is the privately issued document maintained by individuals. Under certain circumstances these are also acceptable as legal proof of birth. How are these certificates generated? Often times families will keep a family record book, many times it is located inside a large family Bible. These were, and still are, quite common in rural areas of the Midwest and the South.

Inside the family record book are birth certificates that can be filled out and signed upon the birth of a child. Often families do just that, particularly if it is an area where the birth may not be registered. One of these certificates, if obviously old and folded and supported by other evidence of identity, will often be accepted as a valid birth certificate. In fact, many people get delayed birth certificates years later based on these records.

The other type of birth certificate common in the United States is the religious baptismal certificate. In areas where the Catholic church is very strong, or other churches that widely practice infant baptism, a baptismal certificate is accepted as readily as a state-issued birth record. In fact, most states and the federal government will accept a valid baptismal certificate as proof of birth.

In order for a baptismal certificate to be accepted as valid, it must have been issued within a few months of the child's birth, it must show the parents' names, the child's birthdate and birthplace, the date of baptism, and show the name and location of the church, and bear the signature and either seal or stamp of the church official issuing the document. But I must caution you again before you go out and purchase a baptismal certificate. Your baptismal certificate should be quite old. After all, it was issued a few months after you were born. A new looking baptismal certificate will definitely arouse questions you do not want.

The new identity seeker has a number of choices when it comes to selecting a new birth record. However, some birth records are better than others in certain situations. When a phony birth record is used, the best situation is to use one that cannot be traced. Here is where hospital and church birth documents have a definite advantage. If you use a hospital birth record from a hospital that has long since closed, the ability of anyone to disprove your record's veracity is next to impossible. The same can be said of deceased midwives or doctors. The same is true if you "become" a pastor in another name and issue your own baptismal certificates. Over the years many churches and parishes have closed down or burned down and the records lost. If you claim a baptismal certificate from one of these services no one can say otherwise. A state issued birth certificate can always be traced to the originator of the record.

All state-issued birth certificates that come from a state's central vital statistics office will contain a state birth number. These numbers are important to be aware of because the Federal Government, in an attempt to reduce passport and Social Security number fraud, has trained its people to recognize these numbers.

First, a state birth number *will not* appear on a certificate issued by a local county registrar. If a person applies for a passport, one of the first checks the Passport Clerk makes is to look at where the state birth certificate was issued. If it came from the state vital statistics office, it should have a birth number on it, and this number is written down on the application form. If it was issued by a county registrar, the certificate will only carry a local registrar's file number on it. Any mismatch will immediately alert the Passport Clerk to possible identity fraud and cause her to retain the certificate.

The United States uses a common system of Birth Certificate numbers due to an agreement reached among the states years ago. It is arranged thusly:

First digit:	always a "1" — shows birth in USA
Next two digits:	represent state of birth: "34" is Ohio
Next two digits:	represent year of birth: "75" is birth in 1975
Last six digits:	state file number, random sequential number

For example: 1/34-75-041171
                     Born in the State of Ohio (34)
                     Born in Year 1975
                     State File 041171

- 8 -

DOCUMENT CERTIFICATION

Everyone always wants *certified* copies of documents. This can be a problem for the identity changer, particularly where it relates to birth certificates. There is often a lot of confusion over the difference between certification and notarization. A *certified* document is one where the *original* issuer of the document attests to its accuracy and validity. When the local county registrar affixes either his stamp or seal and signature onto the document, he is certifying its contents. His certification is saying that the information contained on the front of the document is the same as that contained in the county birth records book.

A notarization seal is something different altogether. If I make a copy of a document and get it notarized, all the notary public's seal and signature means is that the photocopy is a true and accurate photocopy of the actual original document provided. The notary public's seal *does not* attest to the accuracy or validity of the information contained on the original. However, there is a lot of confusion on this matter among the identity bureaucrats themselves. A properly notarized copy of a birth record or baptismal certificate will usually get you past all state-level identity bureaucrats. The only person who can certify a document is the original issuer of the record. However, this opens up a myriad of opportunities.

What should be clear is that if you are going to present a hospital birth record or baptismal record as your proof of birth, you must present either a certified or notarized copy of the original, or suitably age the original document so that it appears to have been issued years ago. A similar procedure can be done with state issued birth certificates as well.

To certify your own documents, you will require a stamp that will have the word "Certified" on it and an embossing tool. You can purchase both of these from office supply or legal supply stores. You will also want an adjustable date stamp. Let's say you are going to certify a hospital-type birth certificate as a midwife or doctor. You would purchase a hospital-type certificate through the mail. Once it arrived you would go to a do-it-yourself copy shop and make three or four photocopies of the certificate. You would want to add a heading to the top of the certificate in bold type or with transfer lettering. This heading might say "Mary McMurdo, Licensed Midwife" or "Dr. Jekyll, M.D., Ob. Gyn." Once this is done, run off the copy onto parchment stock. I prefer blue or green. Once you have done this, you would then enter in the birth particulars. Remember, at the time of your birth, these things were often done by hand or on a manual typewriter. Once you have done this, you would add the witness signatures. Now you are ready to certify the document.

To certify the document, you would take your stamp that says "Certified" and stamp the document somewhere around the lower center or edge. A nice added touch is a bold signature line underneath the "Certified" stamp. You would sign on this line, and then use your date stamp underneath your signature. The coup de grace comes when you take your embossing tool and emboss right around the "certified" stamp and signature. Your embosser should have the initials of the "midwife" or "doctor." You must now age this document so it appears to be old and authentic.

An old document would have many creases across it from having been folded many times. The paper will feel a bit rough and the color will be a bit faded. The edges will be a bit rough and possibly a little frayed. How can we get this look? I call it the shoe technique. Get a small plastic sandwich bag. Carefully fold up your certificate, information side inward, and place it inside the bag. You should fold it small enough so that it will fit comfortably inside your shoe. Wear the certificate alternately between your heel and your toes on both feet for about a week. At the end of the week, remove the certificate from the bag. It will look quite elderly. Another helpful hint is to place it folded inside of a large book, perhaps at night when you are asleep. Anyone who now sees this certificate will believe it is old.

This method of do-it-yourself certification will also work on church-issued baptismal certificates, and even on state-issued birth certificates. The baptismal certificates are the easiest to get. Simply visit any church or religious supply store and look for their baptismal certificates. Try to select one that carries the information on it mentioned earlier. The next step is to decide which church it will be from. You are best advised to use an out of state church that no one in your area would be familiar with. Generally the baptismal certificate will have enough artwork on it so that you must not add any. For good measure, you might wish to run it off onto parchment stock at a quick copy shop.

Once this is done, you would type the data onto the certificate and then do your embossing and certifying job, except in this case your embossing tool might have the church initials on it. You may wish to add the church name and address to the top of the certificate as well. As added security you could pick a church that had closed or burned down years ago. Once again, the document would need to be aged in the way previously described.

Another option for baptismal certificate generation is to become a "minister" with a mail order church. A little explanation is necessary. There are many "churches" that exist in name only. These churches exist primarily by selling new memberships to wanna-be pastors and ministers. By purchasing one of these church charters the holder can then take a vow of poverty to the "church" and not pay income tax on his salary. These churches will also sell you seals, certification stamps and blank baptismal certificates. You could purchase a church charter and set it up in a mail forwarding service in another city. Then you could issue official certified baptismal certificates in the church name.

Another advantage to this route is that you can now issue *certified copies* of your baptismal certificates, and not just worn originals. You would simply run off a copy of the baptismal certificate, minus your church certification, on to a larger sheet of paper. Then you would apply your church stamps and certification seal to the copy. This will then make this copy acceptable to any bureaucrat.

You can make your own certified copies of actual state-issued birth records this same way. The first step is to write and obtain an actual birth certificate from the state of interest. This will allow you to see what type of paper is used and the certificate layout. Some states issue certificates on intaglio printed paper with fancy borders. Others will still issue plain paper certificates, particularly if a birth certificate comes from a local county registrar. Once you have the state certificate, make a good copy of it onto a sheet of plain paper. Carefully white out all of the information on it and remove all state seals and embossing. One way to reduce the amount of covering up you must do is to request an *un*certified copy of a birth record, in addition to a certified one.

Once the certificate has been cleaned up, you would then run it off onto parchment stock, or even onto intaglio bordered paper. After this is done, you would then type on the new data and then certify the certificate. But for this your embossing tool might have the initials DVS or OVS on it. These initials stand for the Department of Vital Statistics or Office of Vital Statistics. On the inside you would do pretty much as before with the "Certified" stamp and signature line, except underneath the signature line you might bold in "UNDER MY HAND, DEPUTY REGISTRAR" and then stamp the date below it. Any bureaucrat presented with this certificate will believe it is the real thing. He will feel for the raised embossed seal and feel it and see the certification stamp and assume that it is the real McCoy.

- 9 -

CHILD SUPPORT
LAWS

In the summer of 1989 the federal government reached an agreement with most of the states regarding child welfare laws. This agreement stated that the federal government would be willing to help enforce state child support orders with information available in federal data banks only if the states agreed to attempt to obtain the Social Security numbers of both parents upon the birth of a child. When the parents are asked to complete the paperwork for the state birth registration, they will find spaces for them to fill in their respective Social Security numbers. The long term implications of this are clear. Everyone who has a child born will have their Social Security numbers recorded and easily available to any state bureaucrat. Soon afterwards, states would probably begin to assign birth certificate numbers or order birth records according to the parent's Social Security number.

How would the federal government use this information? The first step would be for each state to set up a directorate in their child welfare division that would link together electronically all court orders that found a particular parent delinquent against a computerized database of state birth registrations. This would enable an individual state to see if a delinquent parent in their state had a child born in that state, but more importantly, if a child was born in this state to the delinquent parent, to obtain the parent's Social Security number. Obviously, if the delinquent parent is out of state, the state cannot do anything.

This is where the federal government would get involved. The states would send at regular intervals a computer tape with all delinquent parents' names and Social Security numbers to Washington, D.C. The federal government would then compile a master file for all 50 states. This master file of names and Social Security numbers would then be checked against a myriad of federal databanks: The IRS, Social Security, FAA, etc. When a "hit" was made, the federal government would send whatever relevant information a particular database had on that person back to the concerned state to assist in the child support order enforcement.

For example, many people are weekend private pilots. When you apply for your student pilot license, you are asked to furnish your Social Security number along with other personal data. Under this new system these records are now available for use by the state in finding you. But FAA records have nothing to do with child support laws, until now.

When the state receives back the information from the federal government, it can then ask the court in another state to enforce its child support order. Eventually this could expand to include non-government databases. For example, many states regard themselves or the ex-spouse as a Creditor for delinquent child support payments. Many states have implemented "Family Maintenance Enforcement Programs" that legalize this view. It would only be natural then for the states to suggest that this list be given to the large national credit bureaus to cross-check against their files, and then supply whatever information they contain to the state.

I should point out why the Social Security number is so important. In an earlier chapter I explained it, but it is worth repeating. The only truly unique indentifier a person has is his Social Security number. There are many people with the same first, middle and last names, who even have the same birthdate. But unless an error has been made, a properly issued Social Security number is unique. As Americans, we have always prided ourselves on the fact that we need carry no official government identity papers. But the government has done an end run around this by encouraging states and other federal government agencies to request Social Security numbers from the public, even when they have no legal right to do so!

The danger is that over the long term we will become a society where you are possibly guilty until the computer clears your name and number. If present trends continue, we will routinely be screened for being delinquent parents every time we use a state or federal government service. This already occurs in West Germany. All West Germans must carry a magnetically striped, optically readable national identity card. This card is checked against a variety of databases constantly.

When a persons moves, they must register their address with the police. When a German applies for a passport, numerous databases are consulted before it is issued. If someone owes back taxes, a passport can be denied. A person behind on a loan payment can also be denied a passport. The question is, do we want the same system to exist here?

There is also a very real danger when large-scale computer matching is done. Most people are nonchalant about these developments, until a mistake occurs that affects them. For example, let's assume a person made an error in another state when they filled out a form, and wrote your Social Security number on it. Let's also assume this person's name is somewhat similar to yours. Finally, we will assume that this person is late on child support payments, and an enforcement order has been made against them.

When the federal government matches up its files against the state files, they will show that you are this person owing the child support money and that you are using an alias, your real name. This information will be sent to your state. All of a sudden you could find your bank account frozen, your credit rating destroyed and a lot of other things happening, all from a mistake. These types of incidents already occur with some frequency.

That was a hypothetical incident, but there are true cases. In the fall of 1989, it was revealed that the then director of the Social Security Administration had allowed credit card companies to routinely check the name and Social Security numbers of credit card applicants against the files of the Social Security Administration. If a Social Security number did not match, the credit card company would then deny the customer credit. As we know, often government files are filled with errors. But because of the large scale computer matching, these errors can cost someone the ability to get credit. But even worse was the fact that we had private, commercial concerns being allowed to access confidential information in a government database. This was one incident where public ire was aroused and the practice stopped.

- 10 -
LIMITING
IRS THIRD PARTY
REPORTS

The Internal Revenue Service was one of the first government agencies to make extensive use of the Social Security number. As everyone now knows, your Social Security number is the key linchpin in the taxation system. This allows the various income and interest earnings statements about you to be matched up positively. It also allows state income tax departments to receive data from the IRS according to your Social Security number, and arrange their files accordingly.

The threat to privacy from the IRS is now coming from what are called "Third Party" reports. The number of people who must file such reports is increasing rapidly. Third party reports have in the past been filed by your employer, when he sends in your earnings slip to the IRS, people who have had a large capital gain on the sale of property or investments, and people with large amounts of interest income. The IRS has now radically expanded the set of third party reports. Anyone who has an interest bearing bank account is now subject to these reports. Anyone who wins any prize money in a contest or event over a nominal amount is subject to these reports. And of course, there is the 10,000 dollar rub. Any cash transaction of 10,000 dollars or more must be reported.

On all these third party reports one must provide a name and Social Security number. Failure to comply can result in withholding of a certain percentage of interest or income. Even the publisher of this book requires my Social Security number or he must withhold 20% of my royalties. Mind you, the groups that must complete these reports have no choice. The government will very quickly audit and otherwise harass an institution that will not comply.

So the question is, how can one avoid being caught in the world of third party reports? There is nothing wrong with arranging your affairs to create as little a paper trail as possible. On banks accounts you have some options. You could open a non-interest bearing checking account. This will not trigger any third party reports. For your savings account, you could open an account in a Canadian bank. You will get an automated teller card that will allow you to access your Canadian account in the United States, and you could transfer funds into your U.S. checking account that way. On your income tax return, you could then enter your interest income from your Canadian Savings account on the "other income" line of the 1040. You are still playing by the rules, but on your own terms. Or you could do away with U.S. banking altogether. The global networks of automated teller machines allow a person to access bank accounts in Canada, or even Australia, right at home. If you were to go the foreign banking route, you would use the following procedure, which I will describe using Canada as an example.

You would open a Canadian bank account, using the services of a Canadian mail forwarding service to act as your return address. (I suggest you read *Reborn In Canada*, available from Loompanics Unlimited.) You would open a savings and checking account, and a U.S. dollar checking account, if you so desired. When you are paid in the United States, you would cash your checks for cash at the bank they are issued against. You would then purchase a money order (not at that bank) for the amount you want to deposit into your Canadian bank accounts. You would then send the money order to your Canadian bank. I am against the use of checks, and suggest you use money orders to pay your bills. But for the odd check, like to purchase something by mail, you can open a U.S. dollar checking account at a Canadian bank or credit union. These checks you can write in the U.S. like any other. Similar arrangements can be made with banks in other countries, but Canada is the nearest, and all bank accounts are insured, as in the United States.

Financial privacy bears a few more statements. U.S. Supreme Court decisions have basically said that a person has no right and expectation of privacy in banking transactions. Deposit slips, checks, transfer orders, etc. are all open documents, and allow a fast paper trail to be made of a person's life. Always use the following procedures. Decide that no one will learn anything about you from your bank account. This is accomplished by cashing your paychecks at the bank they are written on, and making your deposits and withdrawals in cash. Pay all your bills with money orders from private companies or post office money orders. You should never write a check on your checking account except when taking cash out of the bank.

Third party reports can be reduced if you understand them in the first place. Of course, you will always be subject to at least one of them, your earnings from your work, the W-2, but the others can be eliminated through careful planning. You should still declare your interest income and pay the taxes, but you will do so without creating yet another privacy destroying paper trail.

- 11 -
DRIVING RECORDS DATABASES

Nothing symbolizes Americans' desire for freedom more than the automobile. The government has used this fact to take steps toward creating another database of information on the people. Unlike people in most other countries, most Americans at some point in their lives will either own a car or obtain a drivers license. The federal government would like to be able to tap this wealth of information the states have. But generally, they lack the jurisdiction to do so for the average person. So once again we have the interstate compact as the vehicle to give the federal government what they want.

The interstate agreement in this case is called the National Drivers Register. This registry involves about 40 states. It contains the names of people who have had their drivers licenses revoked. It allows a member state to run a check on the database to see if a license applicant has been denied a license. If so, the new state will refuse to issue one. The database is designed so a person who reverses the order of their first and middle name is caught. The database contains a person's name, birthdate, Social Security number (if available), former state's license number, and reason for license denial and/or revocation.

Before we look at where this could go, we should look at the implications of these interstate agreements. When a state enters into an interstate exchange agreement, it is allowing the data it collected on an individual to be used for other purposes than for which it was collected. The National Drivers Register is a good example. Not only do other states use it, but so do insurance companies, credit companies, and the federal government. The real problem is, once such a database is compiled it takes on a life of its own, and it exists in a sort of legal limbo. The information contained within it is no longer legally subject to a particular state's laws on dissemination, nor is it subject to any meaningful federal control. The Federal Aviation Administration checks the National Drivers Register to match the names and Social Security numbers of the pilots it licenses against the names in the register that have drunk driving convictions. Because the database is not under federal jurisdiction, this information could then be passed on to the others.

Where could this end up? Canada is a good example. All of the provinces of Canada and the Canadian Federal Government are working on creating a single master file database on all drivers within the country. The way it is being compiled is that all provinces are computerizing their driver records back so many years. Then these tapes are sent to the federal government, who then compiles a master list, cross indexing it so that they can chronologically trace a driver's history. A person who had a license in Ontario and then later moved to Alberta and got a license there would never shed his Ontario computer file. The national database would always show the old Ontario license number and driver records.

The next step will be to do the same with vehicle registrations. Once this master file was completed it would be interfaced with the drivers license file. Together the new database could not only permanently display your drivers license history throughout the years, but also what kind of cars you owned over the years — forever. The next step would be to get the various states to agree on a common format of the drivers license number. Odds are this format would be derived from the applicant's Social Security number. Whenever a new license was issued, or an old one updated, it would be entered into this database. The database would be located alongside the National Crime Computer in Canada, and when an officer pulled a car over and ran a license check, he could call up a vastly greater amount of information on the driver than is possible now.

The ultimate use of computerized databases results in something known as Computer Vector Tracing. In the next chapter we will examine Computer Vector Tracing, and most importantly, how the privacy seeker can defeat it, or at the very least mitigate its impact.

- 12 -

COMPUTER VECTOR TRACING

Computer Vector Tracing, in brief, involves the use of all computerized databases in an aggressive constant online authorization process similar to credit card authorization. Except here, what we are authorizing is people, not financial transactions. Essentially what we are saying is, until the computer replies with the answer "no trace" or "no file," a cloud of suspicion remains. But computer vector tracing then goes one step further. It allows for the creation of a file on anyone who interacts with the database. This file then acts as a chronological trace of that person's movements and activities.

Already the FBI has made such proposals. An internal study done by the FBI in 1987 asked the question of why not, because the technology is already available. It was only strong negative reaction from Congress that put a damper on their plans. How would it work? Well, the first step is that the idea must be sold to industry and the public.

The way it will be sold to industry and the public is as a way to cut down on crime and losses. Potentially any industry or group that maintains a computerized database could participate. Like automobile rental companies. Auto rental companies will be told that by linking their computers into the network, they can instantaneously receive any pertinent negative information about a renter. When you were giving the rental clerk at the computer your drivers license and other information, after it was all entered on the computer, he would send it to the national computer in Washington. This information would be checked against the National Crime computer, the National Driver Registry, and other like databases. A few seconds later relevant information would be displayed on the auto rental agent's computer screen. Depending on what was relayed, the car rental could be declined. The dangerous part is what you will not see. A record of the inquiry will be created at the National Computer, and if you never had a file before, one will be created on you. Every time you interacted with a database that was linked to this computer file, your personal file would be updated. For example, school boards will be told it is to their advantage to join because then non-custodial parents who take their children could be caught. So your local principal could be helping to create files on you. Airline companies could do the same, and insurance companies as well. The list goes on and on. Your life will become an open book.

What is even worse is that because this National Database will be created out of a number of interstate agreements, and because of loopholes in federal government data privacy legislation, there will be almost no controls over who has access to this data. This will be combined with what is called "free text association" in computer jargon. Free text association allows a database user to enter a name or a location, or an abstract, and then to retrieve any information under that heading. If someone thinks you drive blue 1983 cars, this could be put into the computer, and the names of all people in the database who do the same will be forthcoming. Further narrowing by location and other data would eventually identify the person or persons that, say, a car company wanted to market to. Rest assured that under such a system the information flow will be two-way.

As usual we are brought to the question of what can a person do about this. For privacy, it means using the methods outlined before, but with a twist. It may very well be in the future that it is impossible to avoid this datafile creation. If these proposals come to pass, sooner or later everyone will have a constantly updated file. Achieving privacy in this type of situation boils down to once again controlling the data that is stored there. You will make a conscious decision as to what the various databases will contain. But before we go on to that, we need to take a quick look at the private databases and how Uncle Sam uses them to check up on people.

- 13 -

PRIVATE COMPUTER DATABASES

Private databanks present the most dangerous threat to privacy. Because they are private creations, the few government laws that exist protecting government created databases do not apply here. The only substantial legislation dealing with private databases concerns credit bureaus, and their obligation to allow people to see their credit report and have inaccurate information removed from it. In Chapter 1, I discussed many of these private databases in detail, particularly the nationwide credit bureaus and the Medical Information Bureau run by the insurance companies. My goal here is to show how these files can be used to create a total picture of a person.

There are additional private databases where significant information is stored on most people. One such database, soon to be available on computer disc, is the City Directory.

Most people have no idea what it is. The City Directory is not the telephone directory. It is compiled by a private company by door to door canvassing. Its pages contain a humungous amount of information. Usually a complete listing under a person's name contains their address, what type of accommodation it is (house or apartment), if the person is a boarder, the person's employer and job description, and telephone number. If someone wants to find out if a person is new to an address, a separate section called "new neighbors" identifies this with an asterisk next to the name at a particular address. All of this information is obtainable by just knowing the name of a person. Even a person who has gone to the trouble of getting an unlisted telephone number can have their privacy disrupted. A parallel book called a "Criss Cross" directory, gives all telephone numbers according to address in a given city. An unlisted number can be found quickly here.

In many cities a new type of database is being compiled by rental landlords. These files contain the names and personal data on all renters, and the landlords could assign negative statements to certain tenants. A tenant who complained too much could find out that he or she is no longer able to rent living accommodations easily. Although rental information bureaus are not as established as credit bureau files, in a few years that that will no longer be the case.

Government agencies can and do make use of private databases. The IRS is notorious for such practices. An example of this is called "Computer Profiling." If the IRS wanted to study tax avoidance of people with incomes over $30,000 a year, they could subscribe to credit bureau services that will profile such neighborhoods in a given city. The next step would then be to merge this information with that contained in the City Directory. This will then create a very large database with most of the required information on an individual. The merged database will contain the name, address, home phone number, and employer of every person. To get the other personal data, such as birthdate and Social Security number, the IRS would run this list against its taxpayer files for the area. The resulting matches will show who has filed a return and who possibly has not.

Of course such a procedure would also produce a significant number of errors. People who are not required to file tax returns, or those who use a permanent address in another state might find themselves the recipients of a computer generated deficiency notice. But the real danger is that all persons will be routinely subjected to such computer scrutiny without their knowledge or consent. Once again this practice will be sold to the public as a way to crack down on tax cheats and big-time drug dealers. The reality is that no drug dealers will be caught through this approach and only a very few tax cheats. But we will all have our privacy reduced once more.

The use of these private data banks by government agencies will continue to proliferate. Eventually a profile of most citizens could be compiled by merging all of the major private databases and running this information against what is contained in a particular government agency's file. The private data snoops are only too happy to help; for them it is a matter of financial gain and nothing more. What is the alternative? Read on.

- 14 -

VITAL RECORDS CROSS-REFERENCING AND THE NEW IDENTITY SEEKER

A specter is haunting new identity seekers... the specter of Vital Records Cross-Referencing. The mere mention of it causes those who are interested in creating a new identity to quake in their boots. The bureaucrats have tried to propose it as a way to end the "problem" of people assuming new identities. Many of those interested in acquiring a second identity automatically assume that widespread vital records cross-referencing means the end of starting over with a "clean slate." Not so at all. We shall see that vital records cross-referencing, when it is done on a widespread basis, is a failure in a nation of our size, and it only affects a certain subset of new identity seekers.

To begin with, vital records cross-referencing will only affect those new identity seekers who must have a verifiable state-issued birth certificate. This is only a small proportion of the new identity seeking population. New identity seekers who have stayed current on the literature realize that most Americans are issued two legally valid birth documents. One is the hospital record of birth, which is submitted to the state to allow for the creation of the state-issued birth record. If a state issued birth record was no longer available for certain individuals, a savvy new identity seeker could create and "age" a hospital birth record.

The basic fact is that a new identity built around a counterfeit birth record, properly backed up by supportive identification will suffice in most cases. The new identity seeker can then obtain all of the state issued identification needed — drivers license, credit cards, state identity card, voter registration card, etc. After a year or so, a passport can even be obtained. So the first question for the new identity seeker, when cross-referencing becomes commonplace, is: must my birth record be verifiable? In most cases, the answer is no.

For those who must have a verifiable birth record, we need to examine how a potential vital records cross-referencing system would or would not work in the United States. Consider the facts. The United States is composed of fifty states, Washington D.C., and five external territories. All of these constituent components, as well as local jurisdictions within them, are able to issue certified birth and death records that are accepted in any other jurisdiction. Each of these jurisdictions has its own procedures and requirements for issuing vital records. In total there are over 7,500 offices authorized to handle and manufacture these records. In some areas these records are considered public documents open to all, in others these records are closed and available only to state workers and other authorized personnel.

In the simple mind of the bureaucrat, nationwide cross-referencing would work like this: When a person died in one state who was born in another state, the state where the person died would send a copy of the death certificate to the state where the person was born. This death certificate would then be physically attached to the birth record. Anyone who later requested this birth certificate would be refused, or made to show cause as to why it should be released. It seems so simple, but the reality is far from it.

Consider yourself. Are you carrying a copy of your birth certificate on your person? Probably not. Most Americans do not carry legal proof of birth on themselves. When a person dies in a hospital, surrounded by family and friends, there are people present who can provide the information as to the person's birth. But this does not include people who die in accidents or catastrophes. One needs to look at how death certificates are issued to get a clearer picture.

When a doctor issues a death certificate he is interested in three primary factors. The first is to make sure that the deceased is actually dead. That is why in most states a licensed physician is required to confirm the death and issue the certificate. The books are full of stories of people who were presumed dead by onlookers or paramedics who were later found to be alive!

The second consideration of the doctor issuing the death certificate is how the person died and when it occurred. If you notice on most death certificates there is a lot of writing in the section marked "causes of death." This information is important for many legal reasons, e.g., life insurance, police investigation, etc. The time of death is also important because the county registrar must record the event as accurately as possible.

The third concern of the physician is making an accurate identification of the victim. This is done initially by comparing any identification on the victim with the body. If someone who knows the victim can be found in a timely fashion, this person serves to buttress the initial identification. If no additional information as to the birthplace of the victim can be found quickly, the *death certificate will be filled out with the information available.*

Many new identity seekers have stumbled upon just this very fact when researching death records for a suitable candidate. Often the death certificate will not contain the birthplace of the deceased, particularly if the deceased died in an accident. This same fact will cause a lot of holes in any future cross-referencing system. But these are not the only holes that will be created.

Before a state will agree to affix another state's death certificate to one of its birth records, a lot of legal conditions must be met. This is because the act of mating these two records together effectively declares this person "dead." The state could face massive amounts of legal damage if it accepts another state's death record and accidentally "kills" someone who is quite alive and well. And rest assured this would happen with some regularity if a nationwide cross-referencing system came into being. There are just too many people with similar names and birthdates to avoid a lot of mix-ups. Secondly, some states will not accept other state's certificates of death as legal records because they will not contain enough information. Clearly the states would have to agree to use a standard issue death certificate form, and use the same death certificate issuance procedures.

Another problem with this system is that, for it to be effective, both the central state vital records office and the local county registrar must be sent a copy of the death record. This also entails a lot of expense, because for every death certificate received, a vital records search would have to be performed at both the state vital records office and the county registrar level to make sure the deceased was actually "born." In addition, to cope with the liability problem mentioned earlier the state receiving the death certificate will probably also want independent confirmation of the death by a relative or friend of the deceased.

As one can imagine a large time delay would be involved in any such nationwide scheme. Even if it was done, this time delay would be on the order of many weeks and would allow any new identity seeker a large "window of opportunity" to procure these records. The prospect of a nationwide database to handle this function is similarly remote. One need only look at the British to get an idea of the fiasco that would result.

The British developed a centralized national voter list back in the 1970's. In theory, the central computer is supposed to know who is authorized to vote. The names of 45 million people are stored on this database, and hundreds of thousands of names are added each year. Inputs into the system can be made at hundreds of offices nationwide. The end result is that the system is notorious for creating people where none exist, and for removing people from the voting rolls who are entitled to vote. This happens because so many people have similar names and birthdates. An active database that is so large and constantly changing is subject to huge amounts of inaccuracy. But it is one thing to tell a person he cannot vote, and quite another to tell him that he has been declared dead!

- 15 -
THE
PRIVACY
SOLUTION

There are two ways a solution to the ever disappearing privacy of people could occur. The first route would be the best one because it would signal a societal commitment to individual privacy. This would consist of a series of laws that expressly forbid government agencies from sharing information on individuals with other agencies, unless there were certain well defined and individual reasons for doing so. Each year all people should be sent a letter by any government agency that has files on a individual, asking that person if they would like to see a copy of whatever information is held. Federal and state government agencies should not be allowed to use private databases to get information on people that they could not get otherwise. At the state level, laws need to be passed that prohibit data-matching between state agencies, and the giving of data to federal agencies through the use of interstate compacts. All such compacts between states should first be subject to a vote by referendum in the states concerned. Finally, use of the Social Security number as an indexing tool should be outlawed.

In the private realm, legislation needs to be enacted that only allows use of credit bureau records when a person applies for credit. Credit checks now can be done on people for all sorts of reasons. Employers often do them on new job applicants, and landlords often do them on prospective tenants. If a job involves access to large amounts of money, say, as a bank manager, or dealing in public security, as an armored car guard, some specific exceptions could be made. But these must be well defined and the applicant must be told beforehand, which is not now the case.

Unfortunately, the likelihood of such laws is slim. Those who collect the data and those who use it are much too powerful. But there are other ways of insuring privacy. One must use the classic methods of alternate identity acquisition with increasing diligence. One solution I propose is what I call the "box within a box." Before I describe it, I should say that when we do go to the computer vector tracing system, it will be the only viable alternative. Essentially, in your real identity you will obtain one piece of "hard" state-issued identification along with some supporting identification. This person will not interact at all with the ever-expanding computer network. You will use your alternative identity to obtain your drivers license, for banking, etc. You will have privacy because you will have decided for yourself at the beginning what these computers will know about you. Through the methods outlined in this book, you will restrict even what the datahounds know about this "person." Unfortunately, this will soon be the only privacy left.

- 16 -

CONCLUSION

I hope that this book has been helpful to all those who seek an alternate identity to regain their privacy, or for those who only wish to understand the vast government record keeping that occurs. In the future, more record keeping on individuals will occur, further reducing our privacy. But any system has its weak spots and flaws, and as long as we have freedom of the press in the United States, these flaws will be exposed. The sad fact is that now privacy is something that must be taken by the individual, and when it is not it will be removed by the government.

- 17 -

RECOMMENDED READING

NEW I.D. IN AMERICA
by Anonymous
Paladin Press
PO Box 1307
Boulder, CO 80306

THE PAPER TRIP I & II
by Barry Reid
Eden Press
PO Box 8410
Fountain Valley, CA 92728

HOW TO DISAPPEAR COMPLETELY AND NEVER BE FOUND
by Doug Richmond
Loompanics Unlimited
PO Box 1197
Port Townsend, WA 98368

THE REAL WORLD OF ALTERNATE I.D. ACQUISITION
by D.P. Rochelle
Paladin Press

HOW TO USE MAIL DROPS FOR PRIVACY AND PROFIT
by Jack Luger
Loompanics Unlimited

UNDERSTANDING U.S. IDENTITY DOCUMENTS
John Q. Newman
Loompanics Unlimited

FRAUDULENT CREDENTIALS
U.S. House of Representatives Report
Loompanics Unlimited

CREDIT: THE CUTTING EDGE
by Scott French
Paladin Press

CONSULAR ANTI-FRAUD HANDBOOK
U.S. Department of State
Paladin Press

PASSPORT AGENT'S MANUAL
U.S. Department of State
Loompanics Unlimited

BIRTH CERTIFICATE FRAUD
U.S. Inspector General
Loompanics Unlimited

SOCIAL SECURITY NUMBER FRAUD
Office of Inspector General
Eden Press

COLLEGE DEGREES BY MAIL (formerly Bear's
Guide To Earning Non-Traditional College Degrees)
by John Bear
Ten Speed Press
PO Box 7123
Berkeley, CA 94707

COMPARATIVE DATA: STATE AND PROVINCIAL LICENSING SYSTEMS
U.S. Department of Transportation
Loompanics Unlimited

VANISH!
by Johnny Yount
Paladin Press

HOW TO STEAL A JOB
by Bill Connors
Morrison Peterson Publishing
PO Box 25130
Honolulu, HI 96825

I.D. CHECKING GUIDE
Drivers License Guide Co.
PO Box 5305
Redwood City, CA 94063

I.D. BY MAIL
by Barry Reid
Eden Press

HOW INTELLIGENCE AGENTS CHANGE THEIR FINGERPRINTS
by William Wilson
Alpha Publications
PO Box 92
Sharon Center, OH 44274

REBORN IN CANADA, Expanded Second Edition
by Trent Sands
Loompanics Unlimited

HEAVY DUTY NEW IDENTITY
by John Q. Newman
Loompanics Unlimited

REBORN OVERSEAS
by Trent Sands
Loompanics Unlimited

REBORN WITH CREDIT
by Trent Sands
Loompanics Unlimited

- APPENDIX ONE: -
MAJOR
U.S.
NEWSPAPERS

Before you can request a birth certificate you will have to research the obituary columns of out of town newspapers. This appendix will provide you with the names and cities of these newspapers. If you do not have access to a major library you can arrange to receive microfilmed copies of older editions through interlibrary loan. Another option is to call or write a major library in the city of interest and find out how much it would cost to receive copies of the obituary records from certain editions of the newspaper.

ALABAMA: *Birmingham News,* Birmingham
ALASKA: *Anchorage Times,* Anchorage
ARIZONA: *Arizona Republic,* Phoenix
ARKANSAS: *Arkansas Gazette,* Little Rock

CALIFORNIA:	*Los Angeles Times,* Los Angeles
	The Chronicle, San Francisco
	The Union, San Diego
COLORADO:	*The Denver Post,* Denver
CONNECTICUT:	*The Courant,* Hartford
WASHINGTON, DC:	*The Washington Post*
FLORIDA:	*The Miami Herald,* Miami
	The Tampa Tribune, Tampa
GEORGIA:	*The Atlanta Constitution,* Atlanta
HAWAII:	*The Star-Bulletin,* Honolulu
ILLINOIS:	*The Chicago Tribune,* Chicago
INDIANA:	*The Indianapolis Star,* Indianapolis
IOWA:	*The Des Moines Register,* Des Moines
KANSAS:	*The Topeka Capitol-Journal,* Topeka
KENTUCKY:	*The Courier Journal,* Louisville
LOUISIANA:	*Times-Picayune,* New Orleans
MAINE:	*The Press Herald,* Portland
MARYLAND:	*Evening Sun,* Baltimore
MASSACHUSETTS:	*The Globe,* Boston
MICHIGAN:	*The Detroit Free Press,* Detroit
MINNESOTA:	*The Star Tribune,* Minneapolis
MISSOURI:	*The Kansas City Times,* Kansas City
	The Post-Dispatch, St. Louis
MONTANA:	*The Billings Gazette,* Billings
NEBRASKA:	*The World-Herald,* Omaha
NEVADA:	*The Review-Journal,* Las Vegas
NEW JERSEY:	*The Star-Ledger,* Newark

NEW MEXICO:	*The Journal,* Albuquerque
NEW YORK:	*The New York Times,* New York City
	The Buffalo News, Buffalo
NORTH CAROLINA:	*The Observer,* Charlotte
NORTH DAKOTA:	*The Bismarck Tribune,* Bismarck
OHIO:	*The Cincinnati Inquirer,* Cincinnati
	The Plain Dealer, Cleveland
OKLAHOMA:	*The Daily Oklahoman,* Oklahoma City
OREGON:	*The Oregonian,* Portland
PENNSYLVANIA:	*The Inquirer,* Philadelphia
	The Press, Pittsburgh
RHODE ISLAND:	*The Providence Journal,* Providence
SOUTH CAROLINA:	*The State,* Columbia
TENNESSEE:	*The Commercial Appeal,* Memphis
TEXAS:	*The Chronicle,* Houston
	The Morning Star, Dallas
UTAH:	*The Tribune,* Salt Lake City
VIRGINIA:	*The Times Dispatch,* Richmond
WASHINGTON:	*The Seattle Times,* Seattle
WISCONSIN:	*The Journal,* Milwaukee

- APPENDIX TWO: -
STATE
VITAL RECORDS
OFFICES

ALABAMA:

Bureau of Vital Statistics
State Department of Public Health
Montgomery, Alabama 36130

ALASKA:

Department of Health
Bureau of Vital Statistics, Pouch H-02G
Juneau, Alaska 99811

AMERICAN SAMOA:

Registrar of Vital Statistics
Government of American Samoa
Pago Pago, American Samoa 96799

ARIZONA:

Vital Records Section
Arizona Department of Health
PO Box 3887
Phoenix, Arizona 85030

ARKANSAS:

Division of Vital Records
Arkansas Department of Health
4815 West Markham Street
Little Rock, Arkansas 72201

CALIFORNIA:

Vital Statistics Section
Department of Health Services
410 "N" Street
Sacramento, California 95814

CANAL ZONE:

Panama Canal Commission
Vital Statistics Clerk
APO Miami, Florida 34011

COLORADO:

Vital Records Section
Colorado Department of Health
4210 East 11th Avenue
Denver, Colorado 80220

CONNECTICUT:

Vital Records Section
State Department of Health Services
150 Washington Street
Hartford, Connecticut 06106

DELAWARE:

Bureau of Vital Statistics
Jesse S. Cooper Building
Dover, Delaware 19901

WASHINGTON DC:

Vital Records Branch
425 "I" Street NW, Room 3009
Washington, DC 20001

FLORIDA:

Department of Health
Office of Vital Statistics
PO Box 210
Jacksonville, Florida 32231

GEORGIA:

Georgia Department of Human Resources
Vital Records Unit, Room 217-H
47 Trinity Avenue SW
Atlanta, Georgia 30334

GUAM:

Office of Vital Statistics
Government of Guam
PO Box 2816
Agana, Guam 96910

HAWAII:

Statistics Office
State Department of Health
PO Box 3378
Honolulu, Hawaii 96801

IDAHO:

Bureau of Vital Statistics
State Department of Public Health, Statehouse
Boise, Idaho 83720

ILLINOIS:

Office of Vital Records
535 West Jefferson Street
Springfield, Illinois 62761

INDIANA:

Division of Vital Records
1330 West Michigan Street
PO Box 1964
Indianapolis, Indiana 46206

IOWA:

Vital Records Section
Lucas State Office Building
Des Moines, Iowa 50319

KANSAS:

Office of Vital Statistics
Forbes Field Building 740
Topeka, Kansas 66620

KENTUCKY:

Office of Vital Statistics
275 East Main Street
Frankfort, Kentucky 40621

LOUISIANA:

Division of Vital Statistics
PO Box 60630
New Orleans, Louisiana 70160

MAINE:

Office of Vital Statistics
Human Services Building Station II
Augusta, Maine 04333

MARYLAND:

Division of Vital Statistics
State Office Building
PO Box 13146
Baltimore, Maryland 21203

MASSACHUSETTS:
>Registry of Vital Records
>150 Tremont Street, Room B-3
>Boston, Massachusetts 02111

MICHIGAN:
>Office of The State Registrar
>Michigan Department of Public Health
>3500 North Logan Street
>Lansing, Michigan 48909

MINNESOTA:
>Section of Vital Statistics
>717 Delaware Street SE
>PO Box 9441
>Minneapolis, Minnesota 55440

MISSISSIPPI:
>Vital Records
>PO Box 1700
>Jackson, Mississippi 39215

MISSOURI:
>Division of Health
>Bureau of Vital Records
>PO Box 570
>Jefferson City, Missouri 65102

MONTANA:
>Bureau of Records and Statistics
>State Department of Health
>Helena, Montana 59620

NEBRASKA:

Bureau of Vital Statistics
PO Box 95007
Lincoln, Nebraska 68509

NEVADA:

Division of Health-Vital Statistics
Capitol Complex
Carson City, Nevada 89710

NEW HAMPSHIRE:

Bureau of Vital Records
Hazen Drive
Concord, New Hampshire 03301

NEW JERSEY:

Bureau of Vital Statistics
CN 360
Trenton, New Jersey 08625

NEW MEXICO:

Vital Statistics Bureau
PO Box 968
Santa Fe, New Mexico 87504

NEW YORK:

Bureau of Vital Records
Tower Building, Empire State Plaza
Albany, New York 12237

NEW YORK CITY:

Bureau of Vital Records
125 Worth Street
New York, New York 10013

NORTH CAROLINA:

Vital Records Branch
PO Box 2091
Raleigh, North Carolina 27602

NORTH DAKOTA:

Division of Vital Records
Office of Statistical Services
Bismarck, North Dakota 58505

OHIO:

Division of Vital Statistics
65 South Front Street
Columbus, Ohio 43215

OKLAHOMA:

Vital Records Section
PO Box 53551
Oklahoma City, Oklahoma 73152

OREGON:

Vital Statistics Section
PO Box 116
Portland, Oregon 97207

PENNSYLVANIA:

Division of Vital Statistics
PO Box 1528
New Castle, Pennsylvania 16103

PUERTO RICO:

Vital Statistics
Department of Health
San Juan, Puerto Rico 00908

RHODE ISLAND:

Division of Vital Statistics
75 Davis Street
Providence, Rhode Island 02908

SOUTH CAROLINA:

Office of Vital Records
600 Bull Street
Columbia, South Carolina 29201

SOUTH DAKOTA:

Health Statistics
Joe Foss Office Building
Pierre, South Dakota 57501

TENNESSEE:

Tennessee Vital Records
Cordell Hull Building
Nashville, Tennessee 37219

TEXAS:

Bureau of Vital Statistics
1100 West 49th Street
Austin, Texas 78756

U.S. VIRGIN ISLANDS:

Registrar of Vital Statistics
(St. Croix)
Charles Harwood Memorial Hospital
St. Croix, U.S. Virgin Islands 00820
(St. Thomas/St. John)
Registrar of Vital Statistics
Charlotte Amalie
St. Thomas, U.S. Virgin Islands 00802

UTAH:

Bureau of Health Statistics
PO Box 2500
Salt Lake City, Utah 84110

VERMONT:

Vital Records Section
Box 70, 60 Main Street
Burlington, Vermont 05402

WASHINGTON:

Vital Records
PO Box 9709, ET-11
Olympia, Washington 98504

WEST VIRGINIA:

Division of Vital Statistics
State Office Building No. 3
Charleston, West Virginia 25305

WISCONSIN:

Bureau of Health Statistics
PO Box 309
Madison, Wisconsin 53701

WYOMING:

Vital Records Section
Hathaway Building
Cheyenne, Wyoming 82002

- APPENDIX THREE: -

SOCIAL SECURITY NUMBER LIST

As part of your identity change you will be required to use a bogus interim Social Security Number. The following list provides a guide to the current number series in use for each state. You will also notice at the bottom of the list, is a group of new number series that are coming into use. These numbers should be avoided. Remember that your Social Security Number should match the "background" that you are trying to present.

Alabama	416-424	Delaware	221-222
Alaska	574	D.C.	577-579
Arizona	526-527	Florida	261-267
Arkansas	429-432	Georgia	252-260
California	545-573	Hawaii	575-576
Colorado	521-524	Idaho	518-519
Connecticut	040-049	Illinois	318-361

Indiana	303-317	South Dakota	503-504
Iowa	478-485	Tennessee	408-415
Kansas	509-515	Texas	449-467
Kentucky	400-407	Utah	528-529
Louisana	433-439	Vermont	008-009
Maine	004-007	Virginia	223-231
Maryland	212-220	Washington	531-539
Massachusetts	010-034	West Virginia	223-231
Michigan	362-386	Wisconsin	387-399
Minnesota	468-477	Wyoming	520
Mississippi	425-428		
Missouri	486-500	**Additions**	
Montana	516-517	Arizona	600-601
Nebraska	505-508	California	602-626
Nevada	530	Florida	589-595
New Hampshire	001-003	Mississippi	587-588
New Jersey	135-158	New Mexico	585
New Mexico	525 & 585	North Carolina	232
New York	050-134		
North Carolina	237-246	**Miscellaneous**	
North Dakota	501-502	Virgin Islands	580
Ohio	268-302	Puerto Rico	580-584
Oklahoma	440-448	Guam, Samoa &	
Oregon	540-544	Pacific Terr.	586
Pennsylvania	159-211	Railroad Ret.	700-728
Rhode Island	035-039		
South Carolina	247-251		

- APPENDIX FOUR: - MOTOR VEHICLE DEPARTMENT ADDRESSES

Before you go to your new state and attempt to obtain a State Identity Card and Drivers License you should first write ahead and request a copy of the drivers booklet. Your cover story will be that you are moving to the state soon and want to prepare for the test early. The return address will be that of your mail forwarding service. This will let you know in advance what types of identification you will need to get the state identity card and drivers license.

ALABAMA:

Department of Public Safety
Drivers License Division
PO Box 1471
Montgomery, Alabama 36192
(205) 261-4400

ALASKA:

Department of Public Safety
Pouch N
Juneau, Alaska 99811
(907) 465-4364

ARIZONA:

Motor Vehicle Division
1801 W Jefferson
Phoenix, Arizona 85009
(602) 255-7723

ARKANSAS:

Office of Driver Services
PO Box 1272
Little Rock, Arkansas 72203
(501) 371-1743

CALIFORNIA:

Department of Motor Vehicles
Division of Drivers Licenses
PO Box 12590
Sacramento, California 95813
(916) 445-6236

COLORADO:

Motor Vehicle Division
140 W 6th Avenue
Denver, Colorado 80204
(303) 866-3407

CONNECTICUT:

Department of Motor Vehicles
60 State Street
Wethersfield, Connecticut 06109
(203) 566-3300

DELAWARE:

Motor Vehicle Division
PO Box 698
Highway Administration Building
Dover, Delaware 19901
(302) 736-4497

DISTRICT OF COLUMBIA:

Department of Motor Vehicles
301 C Street NW
Washington, DC 20001
(202) 727-6679

FLORIDA:

Division of Drivers Licenses
Department of Highway Safety
Neil Kirkman Building
Tallahassee, Florida 32201
(904) 488-3144

GEORGIA:

Department of Public Safety
PO Box 1456
Atlanta, Georgia 30371
(404) 656-5890

HAWAII:
Motor Vehicle Safety Office
Department of Transportation
869 Punchbowl Street
Honolulu, Hawaii 96813
(808) 548-3205/5756

IDAHO:
Motor Vehicle Bureau
PO Box 34
Boise, Idaho 83731
(208) 334-2586

ILLINOIS:
Department of Motor Vehicles
2701 Dirksen Parkway
Springfield, Illinois 62723
(217) 782-6212

INDIANA:
Bureau of Motor Vehicles
Room 4021
State Office Building
Indianapolis, Indiana 46204
(317) 232-2798

IOWA:
Department of Transportation
Office of Drivers License
Lucas State Office Building
Des Moines, Iowa 50319
(515) 281-5649

KANSAS:
Department of Revenue
Division of Vehicles
State Office Building
Topeka, Kansas 66626
(913) 296-3601

KENTUCKY:
Transportation Cabinet
Division of Drivers Licensing
State Office Building
Frankfort, Kentucky 40622
(502) 564-6800

LOUISIANA:
Department of Public Safety
Office of Motor Vehicles
PO Box 64886
Baton Rouge, Louisiana 70896
(504) 925-6343

MAINE:
Secretary of State
Division of Motor Vehicles
Augusta, Maine 04333
(207) 289-3583

MARYLAND:
Motor Vehicle Administration
6601 Ritchie Highway
Glen Burnie, Maryland 21062
(301) 768-7255

MASSACHUSETTS:

Registry of Motor Vehicles
100 Nashua Street
Boston, Massachusetts 02114
(617) 727-3700

MICHIGAN:

Bureau of Driver & Vehicle Records
Secondary Complex
Lansing, Michigan 48918
(517) 322-1460

MINNESOTA:

Drivers License Division
161 Transportation Building
St. Paul, Minnesota 55155
(612) 296-6000

MISSISSIPPI:

Department of Public Safety
PO Box 958
Jackson, Mississippi 39205
(601) 982-1212

MISSOURI:

Drivers License Bureau
PO Box 200
Jefferson City, Missouri 65101
(314) 751-2733

MONTANA:
Drivers Services
303 N Roberts
Helena, Montana 59620
(406) 444-3273

NEBRASKA:
Department of Motor Vehicles
301 Centennial Mall S
PO Box 94789
Lincoln, Nebraska 68509
(402) 471-2281

NEVADA:
Department of Motor Vehicles
Drivers License Division
555 Wright Way
Carson City, Nevada 89711
(702) 885-5360

NEW HAMPSHIRE:
Division of Motor Vehicles
Hazen Drive
Concord, New Hampshire 03301
(603) 271-2371

NEW JERSEY:
Division of Motor Vehicles
25 S Montgomery Street
Trenton, New Jersey 08666
(609) 292-9849

NEW MEXICO:
Motor Vehicle Division
Drivers Service Bureau
Manuel Lujan Sr. Building
Santa Fe, New Mexico 87503
(505) 827-2362

NEW YORK:
License Production Bureau
PO Box 2688
Empire State Plaza
Albany, New York 12220
(518) 474-2068

NORTH CAROLINA:
Division of Motor Vehicles
1100 New Bern Avenue
Raleigh, North Carolina 27697
(919) 733-4241

NORTH DAKOTA:
State License Division
State Highway Building
Capitol Grounds
Bismarck, North Dakota 58505
(701) 224-4353

OHIO:
Bureau of Motor Vehicles
4300 Kimberly Parkway
Columbus, Ohio 43227
(614) 466-7666

OKLAHOMA:
> Department of Public Safety
> 3600 N Eastern
> Oklahoma City, Oklahoma 73136
> (405) 424-0411

OREGON:
> Motor Vehicle Division
> 1905 Lana Avenue NE
> Salem, Oregon 97301
> (503) 378-6994

PENNSYLVANIA:
> Bureau of Drivers Licensing
> Commonwealth & Forstre
> Harrisburg, Pennsylvania 17122
> (717) 787-3130

RHODE ISLAND:
> Division of Motor Vehicles
> State Office Building
> Providence, Rhode Island 02903
> (401) 277-3000

SOUTH CAROLINA:
> Department of Highways &
>   Public Transportation
> Motor Vehicle Division
> Drawer 1498
> Columbia, South Carolina 29216
> (803) 758-3201

SOUTH DAKOTA:

Department of Public Safety
118 W Capitol
Pierre, South Dakota 57501
(605) 773-3191

TENNESSEE:

Department of Safety
Andrew Jackson State
    Office Building
Nashville, Tennessee 37210

TEXAS:

Department of Public Safety
PO Box 4087
5805 N Lamar
Austin, Texas 78773
(512) 465-2000

UTAH:

Department of Public Safety
Drivers License Division
4501 South 2700 W
Salt Lake City, Utah 84119
(801) 965-4400

VERMONT:

Department of Motor Vehicles
Montpelier, Vermont 05602
(802) 828-2121

VIRGINIA:
Department of Motor Vehicles
PO Box 27412
Richmond, Virginia 23269-0001
(804) 257-0406

WASHINGTON:
Department of Licensing
Highways-Licenses Building
Olympia, Washington 98504
(206) 753-6977

WEST VIRGINIA:
Department of Motor Vehicles
1800 Washington Street East
Charleston, West Virginia 25317
(304) 348-2719

WISCONSIN:
Division of Motor Vehicles
4802 Sheboygan Avenue
Madison, Wisconsin 53702
(608) 266-2237

WYOMING:
Motor Vehicle Division
2200 Carey Avenue
Cheyenne, Wyoming 82002
(307) 777-7971

- APPENDIX FIVE: -

MAIL ORDER CHURCHES

Calvary Fellowship Church
316 California Avenue #435
Reno, Nevada 89509

Victory New Testament Followship
PO Box 3731
Dallas, Texas 75208

American Life Church
PO Box 7583
Phoenix, Arizona 85011

Disciples of Divine Rights
Box 7498
Long Island, New York 10027

Also check for ads in:
  National Enquirer
  The Star
  The Globe

- APPENDIX SIX: -

BLANK CERTIFICATE SUPPLIERS

National Certificate Company
210 Fifth Avenue
New York, New York 10010

Cardinal Publishing Company
PO Box 5200
Jacksonville, Florida 32247

Big Bear Press
555 Saturn Blvd, Ste B-430
San Diego, California 92154

Crown Publishing Company
2400 West Coast Highway, Dept. M-38
Newport Beach, California 92663

Ideal Studios
PO Box 41156
Chicago, Illinois 60641

Specialty Document Company
PO Box 5684
El Monte, California 91731

- APPENDIX SEVEN: -

PRINTING SUPPLIES/ STAMPS AND SEALS

Justrite Stamp and Seal Company
1301-T Grand Avenue
Kansas City, Missouri 64106

Salt Lake Stamp Company
380 W 200th South
PO Box 2399
Salt Lake City, Utah 84110

Goes Lithographing Company
41 West 61st Street
Chicago, IL 60621

YOU WILL ALSO WANT TO READ:

☐ **61092 HOW TO USE MAIL DROPS FOR PRIVACY AND PROFIT,** *by Jack Luger.* Mail drops are the number one most important technique for insuring your privacy. They are confidential mailing addresses that allow you to receive and send mail anonymously. This books will show you how choose, use and profit from a mail drop, and much more. *1988, 5½ x 8½, 112 pp, illustrated, soft cover.* **$12.50.**

☐ **61058 METHODS OF DISGUISE,** *by John Sample.* Need a new look to go with your new I.D.? Everything from "quick change" methods to long-term permanent disguises are covered in illustrated detail. Disguise yourself so completely even old friends won't recognize you! *1984, 5½ x 8½, 142 pp, profusely illustrated, soft cover.* **$14.95.**

☐ **61082 HOW TO DISAPPEAR COMPLETELY AND NEVER BE FOUND,** *by Doug Richmond.* Heavy-duty disappearing techniques for those with a "need to know!" This amazing book tells you how to arrange for a new identification, plan for a disappearance, avoid leaving a paper trail, case histories, and more. The author shows you how to pull off a disappearance, and how to stay free and never be found. *1986, 5½ x 8½, 107 pp, soft cover.* **$12.95.**

☐ **61060 THE CRIMINAL USE OF FALSE IDENTIFICATION.** An exact reprinting of the relevant portions of a Congressional investigation into the criminal use of false identification. Covers credit card fraud, welfare fraud, food stamp fraud, using false I.D. for insurance fraud, and much more. *1976, 5½ x 8½, 198 pp, illustrated, soft cover.* **$9.95.**

And much more! We offer the very finest in controversial and unusual books— please turn to our catalog advertisement on the next page.

**Loompanics Unlimited
PO Box 1197
Port Townsend, WA 98368**

USA93

Please send me the books I have checked above. I have enclosed $_____ which includes $4.00 for shipping and handling of 1 to 3 books, $6.00 for 4 or more.

Name_____

Address _____

City _____

State/Zip _____

(Washington residents include 7.8% sales tax.)